ESPN
SPORTSCENTURY

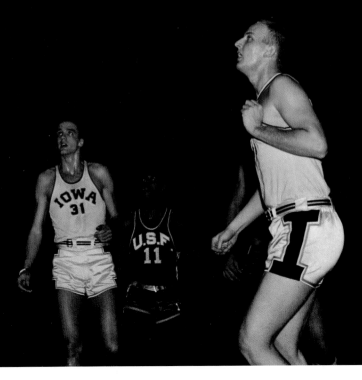

60s

RUSSELL
NOTHING BUT A MAN

RARE AIR MEDIA

ESPN SportsCentury is published by Rare Air Media.

Rare Air Books, a division of Rare Air Media, LTD., is a full service promotional publishing entity with leading edge in-house editorial, design and production capabilities using state-of-the-art technology.

Six volume ESPN Sports Century edition from a concept originated and developed by Jim Muldoon of Food for Thought, in association with Rare Air Books. For additional information, please contact Food for Thought at (516) 331-8063

Rare Air books may be purchased for educational, business, or sales promotional use. For information please contact, Jim Forni at Rare Air Media (773) 342-5180.

FIRST EDITION
Library of Congress Cataloging-in-Publication Data is available from the Publisher.
ISBN 1-892866-10-2
RA 10 9 8 7 6 5 4 3 2 1

DESIGNED AND PRODUCED BY

RARE AIR MEDIA

1711 North Paulina, Suite 311, Chicago, Illinois 60622

TEXT BY

Tony Kornheiser

CONTRIBUTING WRITERS

Michael Point, Mark Rosner, Mark Wangrin, David Zivan

EDITED BY

Michael MacCambridge

PHOTOGRAPHS, PAINTINGS AND ARTIFACTS

All Sport: 24-25, 28
AP/Wide World Photos: 40, 58 (right), 61
Archive Photos: 20, 36-37, 49
Archive Photos/The Sporting News: 21, 27, 39
Vernon J. Biever: 52
The Boston Celtics: 6
Nathaniel S. Butler/NBA Photos: Front Cover
Corbis: 2-3, 4, 9, 11 (top), 11 (bottom), 12 (top), 12 (bottom), 14, 16, 17, 30, 31, 33, 34, 42, 43, 55, 58 (left), 59
Corbis/Bettman: 23

The Everett Collection: 60
Walter Iooss, Jr.: 13, 50
NFL: 63
Art Rickerby: 46
Herb Scharfman/Sports Illustrated: 45
Ted Streshinsky/Corbis: 15
Tony Tomsic: 19
Wide World Photo: 40

1960s

CAUGHT IN THE QUAGMIRE OF AN UNWINNABLE WAR ABROAD AND AN UNFULFILLED PROMISE AT HOME, THE NATION SPENT THE DECADE IN A SCHIZOPHRENIC SPASM OF PLEASURE AND REVULSION. FOR THE FIRST TIME, SPORTS SEEMED OUT OF STEP. YET THE FIELDS OF PLAY STILL SERVED AS METAPHORICAL BATTLEGROUNDS FOR THE PROXY WARS OF THE AGE. IN BOSTON, WHERE RACISM WAS PALPABLE AND INTIMIDATING, ONE MAN CHANGED EVERYTHING. BLESSED WITH KEEN COURT SENSE, A MANIACAL LAUGH AND THE PRICKLY PRIDE OF MISUNDERSTOOD GENIUS, HE WAS AN EXEMPLAR OF THE FIRST GENERATION TO INSIST THAT BLACK WAS BEAUTIFUL.

Bill Russell

NOTHING BUT A MAN

By Tony Kornheiser

It was a jumpy, confusing time. On one hand you had people running around advocating "free love," and on the other, the landscape was littered with the most terrible acts of hate, these assassinations. Each day, it seemed, was spent at the barricades. Each day there was a new cause you expected to throw your body under a bus for. Each day, someone with an issue was demanding to know: Which side are you on?

And so you would think that nobody on these seething college campuses in the Sixties could find time for something as foolish, something as politically inconsequential, as basketball. But on Sunday afternoons, there were some of us who put aside changing the world for a few hours. We gathered in dorm lounges across America to watch the NBA, usually to watch Boston play Philadelphia. More specifically, to watch Bill Russell play Wilt Chamberlain.

Actually, to watch Russell beat Chamberlain.

Though I'm sure Russell didn't beat Chamberlain every Sunday. Just the Sundays I watched.

These were the days before cable television, before satellite dishes made it possible to see every game every night. There were only three networks then, and you could only rarely watch sports on TV. Where I was—in Binghamton, New York, a small city upstate, a few miles north of the Pennsylvania border—you could go a whole season and never see the Knicks on TV. Not like it is now, where you see your home team so often you know when the 11th man got a haircut.

In 1960, the NBA was a league with eight teams, mostly gathered in the Northeast, and none beyond the Mississippi River. By 1980, because of merger, expansion, or absorption, the NBA had more than doubled in size—as had the NFL and the NHL. This was a period of dynamic growth and expansion in American professional sports, the manifest destiny era. Baseball moved to Canada, for God's sakes, and football started eyeing Mexico.

But in the Sixties, the only time you could see the NBA was Sunday afternoons. And the main attraction was Russ and Wilt. Wilt was Goliath. He was 7 foot 1 inch, 290 pounds—huge, strong, and agile. Everybody was terrified of him. Chamberlain put up numbers that nobody, not even Michael Jordan, matched. The most points Jordan ever averaged for a season was 35. Chamberlain surpassed that average five times. One season he averaged an impossible 50.4. Chamberlain is the only man in the history of the NBA to average more than 24 rebounds a game, and he did that three times. One year, to silence critics who said he shot too much, Chamberlain led the NBA in assists. And by his own count, of course, Wilt led the world in scoring women.

Russell, in comparison, was puny. He was 6 feet 9 inches and skinny; he weighed maybe 230 pounds. He had no offensive game to speak of; he never averaged as much as 19 points a game for a season. But defense and rebounding was Russell's side

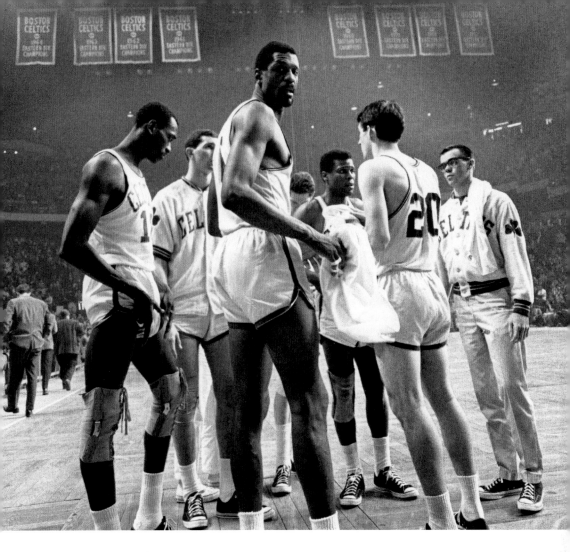

of the street. He blocked shots seemingly at will and always at opportune moments. He swept the boards with a grace and efficiency that stood in sharp contrast to Chamberlain's raw power. Russell played on springy legs, and won with guile and intellect.

Did I mention he won every time?

I have been a sportswriter for 30 years—long enough to know that it is unfair to reduce a team sport to a two-person rivalry. It's fine in tennis to talk about Evert vs. Navratilova, and in golf, to mythologize about Nicklaus vs. Palmer. But you can't cram basketball into that facile equation. There are too many other players on the court. It was never simply Russell vs. Chamberlain.

Yeah, sure.

And now that we are done with that disclaimer: From 1960 through 1969, Russell's team won nine championships; Chamberlain's, one.

If Wilt was larger than life, he was somehow smaller than Russell. Their rivalry appeared to be so one-sided that people tilted toward Russell almost to the point of absurdity. Wilt would get 44 points—there wouldn't be five players all season who'd score 44 points in one game—and people would write: "Russell held Chamberlain to 44."

I sat in a dorm lounge at Harpur College watching these games, thinking that Russell was the coolest cat on earth. The way he handled Chamberlain, it was like he was laughing at him. I watched Russell, wearing that jazzman's goatee—the first player ever to do so—standing slope-shouldered on the court like a saxophone player waiting his turn to blow, then suddenly soaring after the ball like a big black eagle, and I thought: This guy is so cool, he should play in sunglasses.

A couple of thousands of miles across the country, at the University of Missouri, my friend Jack sat in a dorm lounge watching the same games, thinking something murderously different. Jack was from Scranton, Pennsylvania. He loved all the Philadelphia teams. He loved Hal Greer. He loved Paul Arizin before him. And of course he loved Chamberlain—and hated Russell, for those many Sundays when Russell crushed his hope.

It was during this time that the great sportswriter Jim Murray would write:

"Bill Russell is like Wellington to Waterloo. Like Grant to Richmond. Like the Russians to Stalingrad. He is where the war ends."

And my friend Jack watching these games where Boston played Philly, knew, sadly, that this was true.

"The picture I have is of a time-out," Jack recalls. "The 76ers are ahead by one point. The Celtics have the ball, and the camera is focused on their bench. Red Auerbach is explaining what he wants done, and Russell is just staring, focusing on something only he can see, locking it into his mind. And I'm watching this scene, and I'm saying, 'Uh-oh,' knowing that whatever Auerbach is saying, Russell will make it happen. And we are screwed."

Amazingly, in an era when NBA teams routinely scored 115 points a game, Russell made his mark without the ball in his hands. Maybe it's because Bill Russell invented defense. No, that's wrong, because the way Bill Russell played defense has nothing to with the way, say, Pat Riley or Chuck Daly coach defense. Theirs is a defense that punishes the enemy until it gives up the ball; it's ugly, like war, even when it works. But Russell's signature moves—the controlled block or the lightning-quick rebound and outlet pass—were elegant transitions that instantly transformed defense to offense, often before the enemy realized what had happened.

In fact, nobody before or since has played defense the way Russell did. He didn't bend rims—he bent minds.

Russell blocked shots at will, and blocked them not for show—not like the trash-talking egomaniacs of the Nineties who block shots to inflate themselves—but for psychological value. Russell used the blocked shot as a deterrent, to make you fearful of shooting anywhere within his range. He was always lurking, but you never knew when he was going to pounce. He might let you inside, once, twice, even three times, early in a game, encouraging you to believe he could be had, until, when the game was on the line, you went back one more time—and left with the ball in his hands and your heart on the floor. It was like playing Russian Roulette. The chamber with the bullet might be next.

"Russell would jump over you to block your man's shot," said John Thompson, the celebrated Georgetown coach who backed up Russell on the Celtics for a couple of years. "The word with kids now is 'Switch!' But I tell them the word on the Celtics was 'Russ!' You could hear that all over the floor. If your man beat you, all you could hear was people yelling 'Russ!'

"Russell redefined defense, he put the honor in defense. He's the guy who made people think there was something to it. Even Michael Jordan in all his greatness, what did he redefine?"

It made Bill Russell's game irresistible—except to Philly fans and L.A. fans. To the rest of us, though, Russell was Horatio at the bridge. He was the gatekeeper. He was the guy who emphatically said, "No! You can't score at this goal. This goal is my house." Yet there was something refined to his rejection, something superior and all the more maddening. It was almost as if you could hear him cackling as he tapped your shot to Couz or K.C.—as if he knew this was just a game.

N ot to make too much of race—but ever since the Civil War, it has been the most volatile flashpoint of our culture. Most of the world's wars have been fought over religion, but our struggles have always been about race. And like the schoolhouse, the ballot box, and the lunch counter, America's athletic fields were not always open to everybody.

Bill Russell came to the NBA in 1956, less than 10 years after the most significant event in American sports history, when Jackie Robinson integrated major league baseball. Although black athletes were playing in the NBA, the NFL, and baseball, there weren't that many yet. Some teams didn't have any. The Boston Red Sox, for example, were disgracefully slow in signing black players. So Russell was the first black athlete of any consequence in Boston, America's most racially charged big city.

It's intriguing to note that the great Celtics dynasty was fueled by Russell and Red Auerbach, a black and a Jew, two outsiders in clannish, Catholic Boston. You can only imagine how it must have delighted Auerbach, as combative a man as ever prowled a sideline, to build the greatest dynasty of that era, while the patrician-owned Red Sox remained mired in mediocrity despite Ted Williams, the greatest hitter in baseball. And to do it with a black man literally at the center of it all. Beating Boston with Russell must have been even better than beating Philly and L.A. You can picture Auerbach kneeling in a time-out, looking right into Russell's angry eyes and egging him on: "Let's show these Boston Brahmins what we're made of."

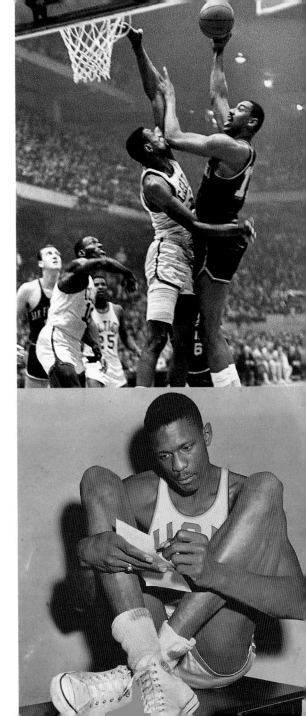

CLASH OF THE TITANS: Russell vs. Chamberlain was the signature sports rivalry of the '60s. Above, Chamberlain hooks over Russell in the '64 NBA Finals.

TOP DON: At San Francisco, under coach Phil Woolpert, Russell—and future teammate K.C. Jones—led USF to consecutive NCAA titles.

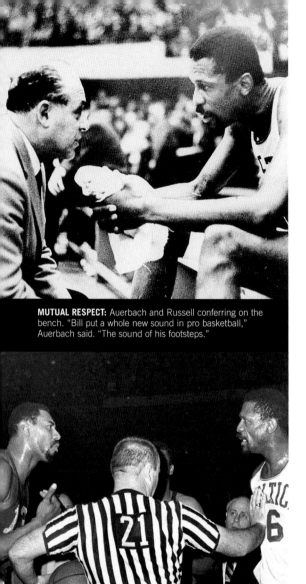

MUTUAL RESPECT: Auerbach and Russell conferring on the bench. "Bill put a whole new sound in pro basketball," Auerbach said. "The sound of his footsteps."

...IN '66: the two nearly come to blows in the East finals. Referee John Vanak holds them apart, while Red Auerbach, behind Russell, prepares to intervene.

Russell was not like Joe Louis, who made whites happy by performing for them and by not agitating for social change. And Russell was not like Robinson, who courageously endured the virus of racism in silence as part of the pact he made with Branch Rickey to be the perfect pioneer and martyr if need be.

Russell represented a new type of black athlete: the educated, outspoken, defiant star seeking—no, expecting—respect just for who he was. In 1961, Russell boycotted an exhibition game in Lexington, Kentucky, when two of his teammates were refused service in a hotel coffee shop. In 1963, Russell was quoted saying, in a *Sports Illustrated* story, "I don't consider anything I've done as contribution to society. I consider playing professional basketball the most shallow thing in the world." And, after being refused food service while on the highway: "Some [black] entertainers try to show whites that they are nice people. All of us are nice people, but this isn't a popularity contest. I don't care if the waitress likes me when I go into a restaurant. All I want is something to eat."

Russell's lineage could be found, not so much in Muhammad Ali—who stood on a separatist platform but craved the love of everybody—but in John Carlos and Tommie Smith, bowing their heads and raising their black-gloved fists on the medal stand at the 1968 Olympics: solemn, dignified, strong, unapproachable. The essence of Russell.

"Russell was the first man I ever heard call himself 'black,'" John Thompson remembered. "This was when it was an insult to call a man 'black,' when it was similar to calling a man a 'nigger.' Bill Russell called himself a black man. He was one of the first men I ever saw to truly acknowledge the fact that he was black, and to identify very strongly with his roots in Africa.

"Russell's manner was so strange and so different. He didn't preach at anyone. He didn't say anything unless he felt infringed upon. But if he felt there was an injustice going on, he'd open up his mouth and say so."

Needless to say, this played better with some whites than with others. Many older, conservative whites found him threatening and thought him ungrateful. Russell was never beloved in Boston—no black man ever has been. But Russell's manner was so calculatedly distant that he wouldn't have been beloved anywhere. It's impossible to believe we'd ever find Russell lighting the Olympic flame, as Ali did, as a sentimental stunt to launch a television spectacle. Russell led his whole life in such a way that nobody would even think to ask.

In those days, to be cool was literally to be as solid as ice—unmoved by what was happening around you, focused only on your goals, unreachable and omnipotent. And Russell was the essence of that kind of cool.

And that cool, deliberate attitude gave him great appeal to young, educated whites, who were discovering black culture and rolling around in it, apparently hoping it would rub off on them. These were the halcyon days of the civil rights movement, after the historic *Brown v. Board of Education* decision and the emotional Birmingham bus boycott. From the mid Fifties through the late Sixties—the years corresponding to Russell's NBA career—black influence would be increasingly felt within the young, white baby boom culture that was so determined to build a better, more egalitarian country than the one they grew up in.

Elvis Presley sang music with a blatant sexual power stolen from black R&B entertainers. White kids couldn't get enough of it. Motown was formed and "crossover" was born; anything with a Motown label went to No. 1. The Beatles and Rolling Stones confessed their adoration for Chuck Berry and Little Richard. James Baldwin became one of white America's favorite authors; Dick Gregory became one of its favorite comedians. And Bill Russell, the NBA's Othello, became its favorite basketball player.

Young whites saw in Russell just what they were looking for: a black basketball player who was an

HALTING START: At right, in Russell's first season as player-coach, 1966-1967, the 76ers and Chamberlain finally broke through to win the title, getting off to a 46-4 start in the regular season. "They're playing the game we've played for the last nine years," said K.C. Jones. "In other words, team ball."

antidote to all racial stereotypes. The game Russell played wasn't instinct and flash, it was intellect and guile. It wasn't basketball at all; in Russell's hands, it was chess. Russell wasn't a dumb jock, he was educated and articulate. He wasn't culturally unaware, he was socially conscious. He wasn't humble and grateful, he was proud and challenging. He was a black man succeeding on his own terms on a team where teamwork was the essence of success. Russell could function within the team and never sacrifice an ounce of originality. Plus, he was doing it in Boston, the roughest racial arena in the league. To many young whites, idolizing Russell became a means of personally redressing the core of racism in their parents' America.

Russell was even more revered in the hippest white enclaves, because they fancied that he was one of them: an outsider and underdog who had to rely on his brains to succeed. How else could you explain Russell's David-like mastery over the Goliath, Chamberlain? Russell was so cool, so aloof; he was like Miles Davis, who was so hip he turned his back on his audiences when he played.

To blacks, Russell was mythic. His ability to win year after year allowed him to push the limits of what a black athlete could acceptably say. In a pantheon of defiant and dignified role models—Malcolm X, John Coltrane, Baldwin, Gregory—

Russell belonged not just for what he did, but for how he did it. And rather than being punished for his stances, Russell was rewarded.

He became the first black head coach in the NBA. How Auerbach must have loved doing that in Boston.

Of course, he paid a price for being Bill Russell. When you hold everyone at arm's length, you never feel anyone's embrace. He was always respected, but never really liked. His refusal to sign autographs angered his critics and confounded his friends. Thompson tells a story of driving with Russell to Maine for an exhibition, and seeing Russell befriend a small boy who attended the game. Thompson watched Russell laugh and joke with the boy, put his arm around him, shake his hand. Then, when Russell and Thompson headed for Russell's car, the woman who had brought the boy to the game asked Russell if he'd sign an autograph for him. And Russell, of course, refused.

BACK TO THE TOP: Russell led the Celtics back to the top in '68, his second year at the helm, coming back from a 3-1 deficit to beat the 76ers in the Eastern Conference finals, then beating the Lakers in the finals.

THE MAN: Russell was the first black head coach in a major American sports league in four decades, but his demeanor didn't change. "I can honestly say that I have never worked to be liked," he once said. "I have worked to be respected."

This was the essence of Russell, of course: caring all for the substance of an experience and not at all for the surface. The rest of the world was left to see things his way—or not. Often it was not. And you wondered whether any of that disapproval penetrated through Russell's outer shell.

"The lady hadn't seen Russ be so caring with the boy," Thompson said. "All she knew was there was no autograph, and she got very annoyed with him. He didn't say a word. He just got in the car and drove off. I said, 'Russ, why wouldn't you sign the autograph for the kid?' And Russell said, 'It has no meaning, having an autograph.' Russell never ever gave me the impression that he cared about what people thought of him. But he had been so kind to this little boy, and the lady had been so huffy with him. I said, 'It must bother you. It must bother you.' And Russell drove on silently."

Thompson idolized Russell. To this day he keeps a pair of Russell's Celtic sneakers on his desk, and a framed picture with a personal inscription by Russell in his office. "I haven't figured him out yet, and I've stopped trying," Thompson says. "Russell always gave me the impression that he didn't want you to enter into his realm of thinking, his realm of space, his realm of anything, unless he invited you in. But if he accepted you into it, he was very kind. People don't know how generous he is."

What Thompson appreciated most about Russell was the secure feeling Russell provided him. Thompson is 6 feet 10 inches, and in those days weighed about 260 pounds. You wouldn't think a man that size would feel intimidated. But back then a black man in Boston walked on shaky ground.

"I always felt safe around Russell as a black person," Thompson recalls. "And I felt very much unsafe with him not around. Here's a guy who comes into the room and just looks like a warrior. He wouldn't be coming in with some polite 'It's nice to meet all of you.' He

THE FINAL VICTORY: Russell and Bailey Howell celebrate after their seventh game win in the '69 Finals at The Forum in Los Angeles. His career ended with one last crucial win over Chamberlain.

wasn't rude. But the way he carried himself was reassuring to me. He came closest to any man I ever met at living on his own terms."

Bill Russell played 13 seasons in the NBA and won 11 championships.

Do the math: Eleven rings. Ten fingers.

The only people close are Sam Jones (10) and Tommy Heinsohn, K.C. Jones and Satch Sanders (eight)—and they all played alongside Russell. Jordan has six. Magic Johnson has five. Larry Bird has three. Add Russell's two NCAA championships, and his gold medal at the 1956 Olympics, and Russell is the greatest winner of all time.

"People can debate who was the greatest performer," says Thompson, "but the greatest winner defines itself."

I believe that some of Russell's more notorious stances—his refusal to sign autographs; his disdaining to accept induction into basketball's Hall of Fame; his frosty, almost contemptuous relationship with the media—may have somehow detracted from what he did. And Russell, as Thompson says, never felt it necessary to explain himself. But you can argue about what you thought of Russell, not about what he accomplished.

Put simply: Russell won. Like nobody ever.

Thompson saw it up close 35 years ago, and is amazed by it still.

"I never saw anybody more competitive than Russell was," Thompson says. "He did not like practice. I remember thinking when I first came to camp, thinking that he wasn't as good as I'd heard he was. He went through the whole camp in a jovial mood, laughing and chatting. So I looked at him, wondering. Then we opened the season in Boston against Detroit, and I was stunned at the change from what I'd seen in practice to what I was seeing in the game. His whole temperament changed. His facial expression changed. His game went to an entirely new level. The minute they threw the ball into the air, I would not have known this was the same man."

Russell raged to win. He burned to win. Despite that cool exterior, Russell burned so much that he threw up before games. His mastery of this rage—his ability to both control it and unleash it at the opportune time—defined the underlying intellect of his game. He never exposed fear, or doubt, or anger, or premature celebration. His demeanor was a constant, as much of a rock for his teammates as his presence under the basket. He could control the basketball game because he could control himself.

When Russell left the game, it was because he no longer raged. "If you are looking for a reason why I feel I have played enough," Russell wrote in *Sports Illustrated*, "I'll tell you this: There are professionals, and there are mercenaries in sports. The difference between them is that the professional is involved. I was never a mercenary. If I continue to play, I become a mercenary, because I am not involved anymore."

It was a bombshell at the time. Boston had just won another championship. It was Russell's third season as coach of the Celtics, and his second straight title. His scoring had dropped precipitously—it was under 10 points per game, though it had never really mattered—but he was still averaging 19 rebounds, and his defense was still ferocious.

To this day, folks think Russell hung up his Number 6 jersey too soon.

But Russell sensed something inside him had changed. It wasn't his ego. The year Russell retired was the year Lew Alcindor was to enter the NBA as the number-one overall pick in the draft; he hadn't yet assumed the name Kareem Abdul-Jabbar or the mantle of the greatest scoring machine in league history. Alcindor was coming off three successive NCAA championships at UCLA, and was so widely regarded as the best player in the world that Russell was asked, "Don't you want to see how you can do against Alcindor?" Russell bristled and replied, "The question is: How would Alcindor do against me?"

He was defensive, as always. Everything Russell did was defensive. No, you will not score on me. No, you will not get inside my head. No, you have nothing to say to me. And so he couldn't hear those who begged him to play on. He listened to the drum in his own soul, and knew that without the rage, he was ordinary. And ordinary was never what Bill Russell was about.

And now, as we celebrate athletes with riches Russell never dreamed of, he has become the whisper of a memory. The Celtics have had Cowens and Bird, and a few more titles; the league has had Magic and Michael, and astronomic growth, though not without cost. It doesn't seem to be so much about winning

anymore. There's too much preening to do—too much yearning to be the man.

Years after Russell was gone, as the story goes, Auerbach walked onto the court at a Celtics practice, and the players were kidding around about who had the best moves, and who had the best shot, and who was the biggest star. And Auerbach waved his hand at them dismissively. "If Number 6 were here," he said, "all you sorry bastards would be shaking in your shoes."

THE COACH: In the '70s, the game would change from the one Russell loved. "I tried to treat them like men," he said of his time coaching the Seattle SuperSonics. "And some of them weren't."

Jim Brown

ALL-EVERYTHING

He'd take off from his three-point stance, moving with power and purpose, take the ball from the quarterback, and burst forward with a brutal confidence, running low to the ground with his head up. And then, at the point of contact, when other runners would cover up or try to fall forward, Jim Brown would explode. Tucking the football tightly to his gut, he'd lower a shoulder toward his tackler, and swing his free arm into his opponent's chest with a stunning forearm shiver. "All you do," said the Giants' feared linebacker Sam Huff, "is grab hold, hang on and wait for help."

For nine seasons, from 1957 through 1965, there wasn't enough help in the world. "For mercurial speed, airy nimbleness, and explosive violence in one package of undistilled evil, there is no other like Mr. Brown," wrote Red Smith. Brown—who lettered in five sports in high school and four at Syracuse University—might have been the most talented all-around athlete of the 20th century. Rather than pursuing multiple sports, he compressed all his talents into football, joined the Cleveland Browns in 1957, and became the best running back in the history of the NFL.

No runner in pro football has done what Brown did for the Browns in those nine seasons. He led the NFL in rushing eight of those years, accumulated 12,312 yards in just 118 games (averaging 104 yards per game for his career), scored 126 touchdowns and gained 5.2 yards per carry, still an NFL career record.

But that doesn't begin to explain the impact that he had on the sport. At 6-foot-2-inches, 230 pounds, he was a fast, intimidating, *angry* runner who delivered as much punishment as he sustained. One Philadelphia newspaperman described him "careening through the Eagles like a runaway taxi in a wax museum."

Though he never wore hip pads, and ran as a marked man throughout his career, Brown never missed a game. After being brought down by gang tackles, he would lie on the ground an extra moment, slowly gather himself up, then gingerly get to his feet. This was his ingenious way of pacing himself; he reasoned that if he moved that deliberately early in the game, by choice, opponents wouldn't detect his fatigue late in the game, when he had to move that slowly.

At the end of the 1962 season, when repeated line plunges cut down his effectiveness, he played a crucial role in a player revolt that got Paul Brown sacked in Cleveland. New coach Blanton Collier installed his option-blocking attack in 1963, sending Brown on more sweeps, and giving him the choice to pick his own holes. He responded by running for a record 1,863 yards and scoring 12 touchdowns. The next year, he led the Browns to their last world championship of the century.

He was dominant again in 1965, winning his second MVP award and scoring 21 touchdowns. And that's how it ended. On the eve of training camp in 1966, while on the set of The Dirty Dozen in London, Brown announced his retirement at age 30. "For all the guys who stayed too long—Joe Louis, Muhammad Ali—I thought it was embarrassing," Brown would say later. "People had sympathy for them, and you should never have sympathy for a champion."

His post-retirement life has been as eventful as his athletic career. There have been numerous charges, but no convictions, of sexual abuse. Yet Brown was undeniably a force for good in urban America. His Black Economic Union helped black-owned businesses in the 1960s. And in the late 1980s his Amer-I-Can Program counseled gangs toward more productive lifestyles. He continued to be outspoken, even threatening an NFL comeback at age 47. "If I became a pawn of society and said the things I was supposed to say as most of your superstars do today, I would be rich and I would be given false popularity. But when history comes down, that ain't nothing. I am a free man within society. I love that."

"All you do is grab hold, hang on, and wait for help"

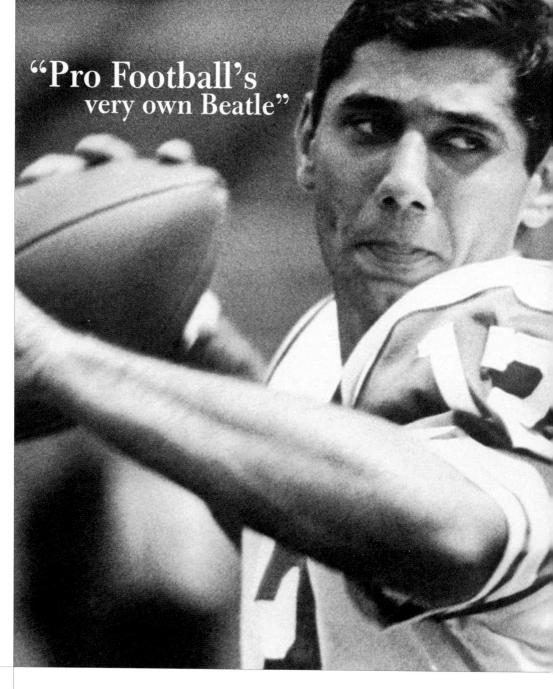

"Pro Football's
very own Beatle"

Joe Namath

BROADWAY

With a quarterback's natural swagger and Sixties sensuality, Joe Namath changed both the structure and climate of pro football. His sleepy-eyed good looks and trademark white shoes made him among the first outright sex symbols in sports—or, as Dan Jenkins put it in 1966, "pro football's very own Beatle." And when he predicted that his Jets would upset the mighty Baltimore Colts in Super Bowl III, then delivered on the claim, he became a legend. Along the way, he fulfilled his ambition "to become known as a good quarterback, not a rich one."

Namath was a three-sport star in high school at Beaver Falls, Pennsylvania, before going to college at Alabama, where he led the Crimson Tide to the national title in 1964, and Bear Bryant called him "the greatest athlete I've ever coached." When the American Football League's New York Jets signed Namath to a three-year contract for $400,000 (twice as large as any pro football contract up to that point), "The Foolish League" forced the NFL toward a merger.

Namath didn't waste any time making his mark on the Big Apple, flaunting both his newfound riches and his playboy image. Whether lounging on the llama-skin rug in his Upper East Side apartment, scrambling through the taverns and clubs of New York City, or marching the Jets down the field in the wide-open AFL, he brought a sense of individualism and style to the game that hadn't existed. In 1967, he explained, "I don't like to date so much as I just like kind of, you know, *run into somethin'*, man." As a quarterback, Namath matured quickly, and by the late Sixties, Vince Lombardi was describing him as "the perfect quarterback." Adept at reading defenses, he possessed a smooth drop-back and quick, almost instant release. ("He makes the rush obsolete," said frustrated Chief Jerry Mays.) Namath became the first quarterback to pass for more than 4,000 yards in a season, in 1967.

But his impact transcended record books. Like Muhammad Ali in boxing, Namath was on the forefront of a new era of great athletes confident enough to boast of their prowess and talented enough to deliver on those outrageous claims. The Thursday before his 19-point underdog Jets battled the Colts in Super Bowl III, he announced matter-of-factly: "We're gonna win. I personally guarantee it." Three days later he engineered the greatest upset in pro football history, befuddling the Colts by eschewing the Jets long-passing attack in favor of a ball-control game plan, made possible by the way Namath artfully sliced up the Colts' strong-side rotating zone defense. Calling audibles on most plays, he completed 17 of 28 passes for 206 yards, won the MVP award, then marched off the field with a raised "Number One" index finger in the air.

The rest of his career would be marked by injuries (five knee surgeries in all) and off-the-field exploits (Pete Rozelle made him give up his ownership of Bachelors III restaurant, and Namath made a memorable television commercial wearing panty-hose). But the league that Namath surveyed at the end of the century was one largely of his own making.

Celebrity aside, when he was healthy, he was among the most feared players in the history of the game. As Raiders owner Al Davis put it in the late Sixties, "He tilts the field."

Sandy Koufax

A LEVEL BEYOND

The right leg stabbed skyward as the body rocked so far back the left hand nearly brushed the ground. It was as much ballet as baseball, but just as hitters became transfixed by the acrobatic grace of the windup, Sandy Koufax delivered the pitch. It might be the fastball, dipping, darting and rising while arriving so rapidly it didn't have time for a nickname. Or perhaps the equally nasty curve, which seemed to start its arc from somewhere out in the parking lot. It really didn't matter because, as Hall of Fame slugger Willie Stargell observed, "Trying to hit him was like trying to drink coffee with a fork."

Koufax was in the majors before he was 20 years old and in the Hall of Fame before he was 40. A late bloomer with a 36–40 record in his first six seasons, Koufax hit his stride in 1961, winning 18 games and the first of his four strikeout titles. Injury slowed his momentum in 1962, but Koufax closed his career in classic style, elevating his art to a legendary plane of performance. Averaging more than 300 strikeouts a season while posting a phenomenal 97–27 record, Koufax was virtually unhittable in his final four seasons as he led the majors in every conceivable pitching category in an unprecedented display of pure and total pitching dominance.

He won just 165 games in his career, but Koufax became the youngest Hall of Fame inductee ever, at age 36, in recognition of the extraordinary achievements and condensed brilliance of his unique, injury-shortened career. He was the first three-time Cy Young winner, and the only one to do it when the title of baseball's premier pitcher went to the single hurler judged to be the best of both leagues. In 1963, when he was also league MVP, he became the first unanimous Cy Young selection, embellishing that accomplishment by leading the Dodgers to a World Series sweep of the Yankees. Yogi Berra, after watching Koufax strike out 23 Yankees in 18 innings, said: "It's easy to see how he won 25 games. What I don't understand is how he lost five."

Koufax's spectacular success came with a physical price, as arthritis twisted his pitching arm out of shape, leaving it a full inch shorter than his right arm by the time he retired at age 30, after the 1966 season. But while pain couldn't keep "our Jewish warrior"—as devoted Brooklyn fans rooting from a continent away dubbed him—off the mound, his faith could. He sat out the opening game of the 1965 World Series to observe Yom Kippur, later throwing two shutouts and winning the final game, along with his second Series MVP award. In the regular season that year, he also established the major-league season strikeout record at 382, and threw a no-hitter for the fourth season in a row, this one a perfect game against the Cubs. Ernie Banks summed up both the game and Koufax's career succinctly: "Sandy tried to throw the ball right past us. And he did."

—*Michael Point*

"Trying to hit him was like trying to drink coffee with a fork"

Arnold Palmer

LEADING THE ARMY

He came charging up the last two fairways at Augusta National, making birdies and winning the 1960 Masters like a John Wayne in spikes. Arnold Palmer began changing golf forever that day, making an elitist sport more inclusive, affecting the game far beyond his 60 career victories on the PGA tour.

Over the next half decade, Palmer became the most popular golfer ever. It wasn't just that he won seven major championships between 1958 and 1964. It was *how* Palmer won, the way he looked more like a linebacker than a golfer, and the timing of his ascension, linked forever to golf's emergence on television and to his rival, Jack Nicklaus. Thanks to Palmer, the number of public courses increased dramatically, as golf became popular recreation for truck drivers as well as doctors. He himself became a conglomerate with the help of super agent Mark McCormack, the first athlete to make millions of dollars from his name off the field.

Palmer introduced himself to America by winning the 1958 Masters, an event televised that year for only the third time. By then, some had already taken notice. At a previous Masters, the writer Dan Jenkins wondered aloud who the vacationing longshoreman was. At 5-foot-11-inches, 180 pounds, Palmer had broad shoulders, a slim waist, outsized hands and muscles developed by maneuvering a tractor at the nine-hole course in Latrobe, Pennsylvania, where his father, Deacon, was once the greenskeeper and later head pro.

With his hair tousled and shirttail flapping, Palmer slashed forcefully at the ball, producing low hooks, often

dramatic ones from the rough after errant tee shots. He chain-smoked, hitched his pants, took risks with his shots, watching them through squinting eyes. He oozed emotion, bonding with his swelling galleries, "Arnie's Army." "Trying to follow Palmer down the course was not unlike running before the bulls at Pamplona," the writer George Plimpton once said.

It was like that at the 1960 Masters. Trailing Ken Venturi by one stroke, Palmer, using his unconventional knock-kneed stance, sank a 27-foot putt for birdie on the 71st hole. Then he hit a six-iron into the wind, leaving himself a 5-foot birdie putt for victory. "If I ever had to have one putt to win a title," Bobby Jones once said, "I'd rather have Arnold Palmer hit it for me than anyone I ever saw."

Palmer's next big conquest was at the 1960 U.S. Open at Cherry Hills, where he trailed Mike Souchak by seven shots beginning the final round. Palmer drove the par-4 first hole, birdied six of the first seven, shot 65 and won by two strokes.

Soon Nicklaus would come; later Palmer's putting would go. The two developed a rivalry born of respect and envy, Palmer for Nicklaus' talent, Nicklaus for Palmer's popularity.

Palmer led the 1966 Open by seven shots with nine holes left. He squandered the lead, lost a playoff to Billy Casper—and became even more likable, more human. Palmer's popularity was built to last, much like the baseball icon Joe DiMaggio. The two-way flow of love has never subsided, as was apparent after Palmer underwent surgery for prostate cancer in January 1997. Or when he approached the 18th green at his final U.S. Open in 1994 at Oakmont, not far from Latrobe. Applause shook the grounds that day, and Arnold Palmer wept.

—*Mark Rosner*

"Following Palmer
down the course was not unlike
running before the bulls at Pamplona"

Oscar Robertson

THE BIG O

Oscar Robertson redefined the point guard position the day he moved into the NBA. With his arrival in 1960, Robertson instantly became the most versatile player the league had seen. At 6-foot-5-inches, 220 pounds, he could shoot, drive, pass, rebound and defend. Not that his domination should have been unexpected: In college, he had averaged 33.8 points, 15 rebounds and seven assists for Cincinnati, becoming the first player in NCAA history to lead the nation in scoring three straight seasons.

Magic Johnson made the triple-double his personal statistical category during the 1980s, but Robertson invented it. He is the only player in NBA history to *average* double figures in scoring, rebounds and assists for an entire season (1961–62). Robertson scored more points than any guard except Michael Jordan, and ranks third in assists after John Stockton and Johnson. "He controls everything out there, and he wastes the least amount of effort of any player I've ever seen," Celtics coach Red Auerbach once said.

Too big for guards to cover, Robertson patiently took advantage of smaller defenders, dribbling forcefully as he backed opponents toward the basket, reducing the distance of any shot by a few feet, then holding the ball high on his distinctive-looking jumper. "He cradled the ball in his right hand like a waiter carrying a tray of champagne glasses," wrote Robertson biographer Ira Berkow.

For all he accomplished in Cincinnati, Robertson never won an NBA championship during 10 years with the Royals. After failing to mesh with his new coach, backcourt legend Bob Cousy, Robertson was traded to Milwaukee in 1970, at age 31. In his first season with the Bucks, playing with the young Lew Alcindor, Robertson finally won his only title.

Considered a warm person away from the court, Robertson often sulked on it, upset with the imperfection of referees, teammates or himself. The first African-American basketball player at the University of Cincinnati, he was deeply affected by the racism he encountered in distant cities as well as his own. Turned away from the team's hotel during a 1958 road trip to Houston, Robertson had to stay in a college dormitory at Texas Southern. "When a black man breaks a window with a brick, America sees the black race doing it," he said in 1968. "But when a white man gets up on a tower in Texas and starts shooting people, then they say it's an isolated case."

For all his oncourt skills, Robertson's biggest assist came long after his retirement. In 1997, he made headlines again by donating a kidney to his 33-year-old daughter, Tia, saving her life.

—Mark Rosner

"He controls **everything** out there"

"The French called her
the Black Pearl"

Wilma Rudolph

GRACE IN MOTION

"T he only thing I ever wanted when I was a child was to be normal," Wilma Rudolph remembered as an adult. "To be average." But the century's most improbable great athlete was never average. Growing up poor, frail and sickly, the premature baby (weighing 4 1/2 pounds at birth) was stricken with polio at age four, leaving her left leg paralyzed. She learned to walk only with leg braces, suffering bouts of double pneumonia and scarlet fever during a childhood marked by almost constant physical therapy.

Finally able to attend school at age seven, she was able to shed her braces for corrective shoes at eight, and three years later began playing basketball in the backyard. By her sophomore year at Burt High School in Clarksville, Tennessee, she was already an athletic miracle, an all-state basketball player averaging more than 30 points a game. While playing basketball, she was discovered by Ed Temple, the track coach at Tennessee State, who presided over the famed Tigerbelles, the nation's premier track and field program for women. Rudolph fell under Temple's tutelage, and suddenly the legs that had prevented her from being normal helped render her extraordinary. She developed into a tall, graceful beauty, 5-foot-11-inches and 130 pounds, with a serene countenance and a quiet determination forged out of her difficult childhood.

When she burst into the national consciousness, after winning three sprint gold medals at the 1960 Olympics in Rome, she became an overnight embodiment of the American Dream. Running with a smooth fluidity, she exuded an economical grace, and even her name lacked sharp consonant edges. Her beauty and success signaled the end of that old shibboleth that women could not be both athletic and feminine.

With her close-cropped hair, smooth smile and gently searching eyes, Rudolph possessed "a look of mingled graciousness and hauteur that suggests a duchess," wrote Barbara Heilmann in *Sports Illustrated*. That distinctive carriage led to her world-wide celebrity, as crowds around Europe clawed to get a touch of her, going so far as stealing her shoes from her feet. The French called her *La Perle Noire*, the "Black Pearl." To the Italians, she was *La Gazella Nera*, the "Black Gazelle."

In America, she was acutely conscious of being black. When the city fathers of Clarksville wanted to throw her a parade and banquet upon her return from Rome, she insisted that it be integrated. In so doing, Rudolph directly brought about the first integrated public event in the history of Clarksville.

She would retire from track in 1963, secure in her accomplishments, becoming a schoolteacher and an inspiration to thousands of athletes. She died in 1994 of a brain tumor, one of the most loved and revered female athletes ever. In 1989, she told the *Chicago Tribune*, "Believe me, the reward is not so great without the struggle. I have spent a lifetime trying to share what it has meant to be a woman first in the world of sports so that the other young women have a chance to reach their dreams."

Gale Sayers

THE ORIGINAL "MAGIC"

H is essence is reflected more in the grainy images from a projector than by the record book, though Gale Sayers did produce jarring numbers. He was a five-time All-Pro who set eight NFL records, and at 34 became the youngest player ever inducted into the Pro Football Hall of Fame.

Perhaps the most amazing number was five—the number of seasons he played before knee injuries took their toll; athletically speaking, he lived fast and died young. "The record book and a thousand feet of action film are all the proof needed of his football greatness," George Halas, the crusty owner of the Chicago Bears, once said.

Yet Sayers wasn't about numbers at all. His career rushing total was only 4,956 yards, and he played in just 68 games over seven injury-plagued years with the Bears, mute testimony that it wasn't what he did but how he did it. With speed and the elusiveness of a bar of soap in the tub, he was Barry Sanders but without the portfolio—and, most sadly, without the benefit of modern orthopedic techniques that could have saved a career ruined by two major knee surgeries.

His nickname was "Black Magic," later just "Magic," because of his supernatural combination of speed and maneuverability. Sayers attributed his edge to how he planted, cutting on his heels rather than the balls of his feet, but this middle son of an Omaha, Nebraska, car polisher wasn't all sparkle and shine. "I hit him so hard I thought my shoulder must have busted him in two," 300-pound Rosey Grier once said. "I heard a roar from the crowd and figured he had fumbled, so I started scrambling around looking for the loose ball. But there was no ball—and Sayers was gone."

"The record book and a thousand feet of action film"

As a rookie from Kansas in 1965, he ran for 867 yards and scored 22 touchdowns, an NFL single-season record that stood for a decade and remains the rookie mark. Six of them came on a muddy field against the 49ers, the last on an 85-yard punt return.

It was the knees, finally, that did him in. A submarine tackle by San Francisco's Kermit Alexander in 1968 tore his medial collateral ligament in three places. After a comeback, which defied medical convention, he rushed for a league-leading 1,032 yards in 1969 and earned the Halas Award for courage, which he tearfully dedicated to his teammate and roommate, Brian Piccolo, who at that moment lay dying from lung cancer. Sayers tore up his knee again in 1970, and this time he couldn't come back. The Magic was gone, and before the 1972 season, Sayers retired.

—*Mark Wangrin*

Elgin Baylor

AVIATION PIONEER

Long before Michael Jordan claimed the air as his performance space, Elgin Baylor went up and checked out the property. Baylor, after a storied college career at Seattle, joined the Minneapolis Lakers in 1958, bringing to the NBA a rare combination of power, speed, grace, elevation and accuracy. He scored with style, flourishing during an era before the NBA's widespread popularity. Longtime students of the game saw a lineage of regal, fluid athleticism begin with Baylor and extend through Julius Erving to Michael Jordan.

In 1960, the 6-foot-5-inch, 225-pound Baylor scored 71 points against the Knicks. For his 14-year career, he averaged 27.4 points and 13.5 rebounds a game. His legacy, seen in latter-day skywalkers Connie Hawkins and David Thompson, would have been even more prominent had Baylor not spent half of his career hobbled by injuries to both knees. Still, he averaged more points than everyone in NBA history save Jordan and Wilt Chamberlain. And no one Baylor's size, not even Charles Barkley, grabbed more rebounds per game. "Elgin is bull-strong, quick and very daring," teammate Jerry West once said. "I think he's the most spectacular shooter the game has ever known."

Baylor had the skill and agility to advance the ball up court like a guard against pressure defenses. Yet he did not avoid tangling with larger players near the basket. Indeed, he enjoyed competing against the great Celtics' 6-foot-9-inch center Bill Russell, contending for tip-offs, wrestling for rebounds or freezing him with moves and shooting over him. Against smaller opponents Baylor didn't have to bother with fakes. He bullied his way to the basket. "When Baylor gets the ball, the opposition scatters like quail at the sight of a hunter," Jim Murray wrote in 1961. But he never did bag an NBA title. The Lakers, led by West and Baylor, lost to Boston in the Finals five times between 1962 and 1968. After Wilt Chamberlain joined the Lakers, giving them three future Hall of Famers, they lost in the 1969 Finals to Boston and the next year to New York.

Baylor could be as formidable off the court as on, needling teammates, rarely conceding an argument. "Elgin was a motor mouth," teammate Hot Rod Hundley once said. "Elgin never shut up." He did on at least one occasion. In January 1959, his rookie season, the Lakers were in Charleston, West Virginia, for a game against Cincinnati. The hotel clerk looked at Baylor and two other African-Americans on the team and said, "We can't take those three. We run a respectable hotel." Baylor said nothing. But he decided to not play in the game. Hundley, a white man raised in Charleston, tried to dissuade Baylor from his protest. When he finally spoke, Baylor said, "Rod, I'm a human being. I'm not an animal put in a cage and let out for the show." Hundley, understanding the dignity and pride in Baylor, said, "Baby, don't play."

—*Mark Rosner*

"The most spectacular shooter the game has ever known"

"It felt like a regular jump"

Bob Beamon

ONE SHINING MOMENT

In the light, tense air of Mexico City, at 3:46 p.m., October 18, 1968, in a few seconds of spectacular physical exertion, Bob Beamon performed what many regard as the single most surpassing athletic feat of the century.

Before that moment the wispy-thin, 160-pound national long-jump champion had traced a strange path to Mexico. His father was dead before he was born, his mother died before his first birthday and his stepfather was an ex-convict, so Beamon grew up tough and insecure on the hard streets of Jamaica, New York. Passing on a scholarship offer from Southern Cal, he started college at North Carolina A&T, then transferred to Texas–El Paso, but was suspended when he and several teammates refused to compete against Brigham Young University due to the racial policies of the Mormon church.

He arrived at the 1968 Summer Olympics in Mexico City as one of the co-favorites, but the smart money was elsewhere. Beamon didn't seem to have the discipline, didn't even make the customary tick marks on the runway to calibrate his strides in the approach to the takeoff board.

But at the finals, preparing for his first jump, he stood at the beginning of his approach and looked up twice, thinking to himself, "Don't foul." He began uncoiling his long 6-foot-3-inch frame over the 134-foot approach, eventually nearing the limit of his sprinter's speed, before hitting the takeoff block perfectly, exploding out and up above the pit.

"It felt like a regular jump," said Beamon afterward. But the leap itself, along with his perfect sprint, form at takeoff, and splendid extension, created something much more: an instant of pure, unalloyed physical splendor. Jesse Owens, who'd once held the record in the event, remembered watching him in midair and marveling at the flight. Beamon came down with such force that he launched himself right out of the back of pit. There was the long wait to measure the jump, as the optical measuring device, moving toward Beamon's mark in the sand, fell off the end of its rail.

The world record at the time was 27 feet, 4¾ inches, a mark that had been extended just 8½ inches in the previous 33 years. But in an instant, Beamon added nearly two feet to the record, jumping 29 feet, 2½. As Coles Phinizy wrote in *Sports Illustrated*, Beamon "had taken off into thin air in the year 1968 and landed somewhere in the next century." On the sidelines, the reaction ranged from awe to anger. "Compared to this jump, we are as children," said the glum Soviet Igor Ter-Ovanesyan. "I can't go on, we'll all look silly," said defending Olympic champion Lynn Davies, before barking at Beamon: "You have destroyed this event."

For Beamon himself, there could be no second act. He would never reach 27 feet again. But 23 years later, when Mike Powell finally bested Beamon's record, it was the oldest mark in the track and field record book. And his legend would outlive even the record.

Dick Butkus

THE MADMAN

They were safe, or should have been, on their team bus after an afternoon of mayhem at Wrigley Field in the late 1960s, but then some impatient driver bumped them from behind in the post-game traffic crunch and one shell-shocked Baltimore Colt couldn't help himself.

"There's Butkus again," came a voice from the rear.

Dick Butkus didn't just hit halfbacks harder, roam the sidelines better and play with more single-mindedness than anyone else, he got into your head. Facemasks were but a hindrance. If he wanted to stick his finger in your eye, he did. If you retaliated, you might start needing two hands to count to five. "That's dangerous for a guy to do, 'cause I got sharp teeth, heh, heh," he once said.

Madness was his method. With fierce eyes underscored with eye black and a toothy, diabolical snarl, he challenged whole sidelines to fights and called time-out late in one-sided games so he would have more chances to hit somebody. He once got four personal foul penalties in an exhibition game. And a poll of NFL quarterbacks named him the second-most-feared defender in the league—21 years after he had retired.

"Butkus, if he doesn't tackle you himself, you can hear him coming," said Steelers quarterback Terry Hanratty. "You know he's going to be there eventually." Bart Starr was more succinct: "Dick rattles your brains when he tackles you."

The seventh of nine children born to Lithuanian parents on the hardscrabble South Side of Chicago, Butkus was a two-way star at Illinois before joining the Chicago Bears as a first-round draft choice in 1965. At 6 foot 3 inches, 245 pounds, he had the size of a defensive tackle and the speed of a running back.

"Dick rattles your brains when he tackles you"

Adolph Schultz may have serendipitously created the middle linebacker spot while playing for Michigan in 1905—he wanted a better view of the offense—but Butkus did for the linebacker prototype what Goddard did for rockets. "If God ever designed a man to be a professional football player," George Halas said, "he had Butkus in mind."

Though he played on only two winning teams in nine years with the Bears, Butkus became the best and most feared middle linebacker in the game, making All-NFL seven times and earning a spot on the NFL's 75th anniversary team. After bad knees drove him to retirement, he became a broadcaster, light beer pitchman and actor, capitalizing on and even mocking his fierce image.

"People feared him, even his teammates feared him," teammate Gale Sayers said. "He hit me as hard in practice as anyone ever did in a game. That's the way he played."

—*Mark Wangrin*

Wilt Chamberlain

ABOVE THE CROWD

Wilt Chamberlain was the first of the giant basketball icons. At 7-foot-1 and 275 pounds, he was the most physically imposing man of his era and, in his prime, the most dominating offensive player of any period. Yet as proficient as he was, the agile Chamberlain could never elude his critics or his nemesis, Bill Russell of the Boston Celtics.

Chamberlain arrived in the NBA in 1959 with a large reputation, having averaged 29.9 points a game during two seasons at the University of Kansas. After a one-year stint with the Harlem Globetrotters, he became even more prolific as a pro, scoring 37.6 points a game as a rookie with Philadelphia and averaging 50.4 two seasons later, an NBA record that stands today. Chamberlain averaged nearly 40 points a game during his first seven seasons, before he decided to become a passer. In the second phase of his career, he became the only center to lead the league in assists during a season. He still holds rebounding records for a game (55), season (27.2) and career (22.9).

Chamberlain's look—muscular upper body and trademark goatee—was as distinctive as his game. He leaned toward the basket for dunks and finger rolls, and faded away for his famous bank shot from the left side. Chamberlain and the 6-foot-9-inch Russell created the league's first great rivalry. It was a source of frustration for Chamberlain, because whatever team he was on usually lost important games to Russell's Celtics. Despite his accomplishments, Chamberlain was frequently attacked by critics, because his teams rarely met their expectations. "Nobody loves Goliath," said Alex Hannum, one of Chamberlain's coaches.

Goliath had one glaring weakness. He was a pitiful 51 percent career free-throw shooter. But Chamberlain made a remarkable 28 of 32 while scoring his record 100 points against the Knicks in 1962. The game was witnessed by only 4,124 fans in Hershey, Pennsylvania, the gym half full.

Though Chamberlain doubled Russell's scoring average, he was almost always compared unfavorably because Russell's more talented Celtics won 11 NBA titles. Chamberlain won one with Philly (1967) while Russell was playing and another with the Lakers (1972) after Russell retired. Boston coach Red Auerbach, who always infuriated Chamberlain, once said, "Bill was a better player because he played with his head, was more motivated and, most of all, had a bigger heart."

Denied titles, Chamberlain took pride in his prowess elsewhere. In his autobiography, he claimed to have slept with 20,000 women and fought off an attacking mountain lion. But years later, the Russell comparisons still evoked a defensive reaction: "Russell didn't win 11 championships. He played on a team that won 11 championships. I wonder how Russell would have rated if his team hadn't won all those championships."

—Mark Rosner

"Nobody **loves** Goliath"

"Talking to A.J.
when he's angry is like
dancing with
a chainsaw"

A.J. Foyt

AN URGE TO EXCEL

A.J. Foyt didn't necessarily want to set speed records, although he routinely did so; he just couldn't bear to have anyone finishing in front of him.

"There never has been a driver with such an absolute urge to excel, the absolute necessity to win," said rival Al Unser. The tough-talking Texan with the turbo-charged temper did exactly that, bringing auto racing into the mainstream of American sports while consistently leaving his competition in the rearview mirror.

Foyt was racing roadsters, motorcycles and midget cars competitively in Houston by his teenage years, eventually dropping out of school to devote his full attention to professional racing. In 1961, three years after qualifying in his initial attempt, the 26-year-old Foyt won his first Indy 500 crown, setting a track speed record while nursing his car home with a defective clutch. Repeating the feat with wins in 1964 and 1967, he solidified his claim as the decade's most successful driver. And in 1977, Foyt took yet another victory lap at the Brickyard, becoming the first driver to win four Indy 500s.

Foyt's success ranged far from Indy and ovals. He won the Daytona 500 in 1972, in the process setting a speed record which lasted until 1980. Even more impressive was his 1967 season, when he won his fifth overall USAC crown as well as winning his third Indy championship and co-driving the winning car in Europe's 24 Hours of Le Mans Grand Prix endurance race.

When Foyt wasn't in front he wasn't much fun to be around. His own father said: "Talking to A.J. when he's angry is like dancing with a chainsaw." Unfortunately, the perfectionist Foyt was angry too much of the time. His public exhibitions of rage, which included punching matches with fellow drivers and his own crew, reinforced his reputation as a rugged, no-nonsense competitor with the explosive temper of a man who just couldn't understand why everyone wasn't as totally focused as he was.

Foyt also possessed an obstinate attitude regarding change at a time when new ideas regarding design and technology were radically reconfiguring his sport. Although he frequently appeared to be racing antiques and was seemingly always behind the technological curve, Foyt somehow still consistently managed to be in front of the pack when the checkered flag was waved.

Retiring from driving in 1993 to concentrate on team ownership, Foyt remained a combative and controversial force in racing. His legacy as a relentless and resourceful driving champion is an illustrious one, as was the individualistic approach he brought to racing. When the indomitable Foyt was behind the wheel, it wasn't the power of the engine that mattered most, it was the willpower of the driver.

—*Michael Point*

Mario Andretti

THAT BURNING DESIRE

They always used to say, 'Man, if the kid survives, he'll be good,'" remembered Mario Andretti of his early days in racing. "That was music to my ears because I knew what they thought: 'At least he stands on the button, so as soon as he learns how to do it right, he'll really go.' You have to show that burning desire. When you do that, nobody faults you."

As a driver, Andretti's desire and versatility were unsurpassed. He arrived in the United States at age 15, from a displaced persons camp in Italy where he'd dreamed of racing greatness, and by the age of 30, he had won both the Indianapolis 500 and the Daytona 500. Later, he'd go on to win the world driving championship in Formula One, becoming the first person to win Indy, Daytona and Formula One and establishing himself as the most versatile driver in auto racing history.

Squinting under his trademark shiny silver helmet with the blazing red arrow on the crown, the compact, 5-foot-5-inch, 140-pound Andretti excelled on dirt tracks, ovals or road races, and he thrived in any kind of machine, from stock cars to the aerodynamic open-wheel racers on the Indy and Formula One circuits. "Mario is the best all-round driver I've ever had," said Roger Penske in 1977. "He's a racer's racer—completely dedicated, single-minded and passionately competitive."

Andretti's father, Alvise, was a prosperous farm administrator in Montona, Italy, who lost his land in World War II, and wound up in a displaced persons camp in Lucca for seven years. Andretti grew up idolizing Italian Grand Prix champion Alberto Ascari. Providentially, when the family sailed to America in 1955, Alvise Andretti found work at a textile mill near the racing hotbed of Nazareth, Pennsylvania, where Mario and his twin brother, Aldo, discovered American sprint racing. Throughout the 1960s, after Aldo was sidelined by a crash, Mario raced whenever and in

"He's a racer's racer—
completely dedicated"

whatever he could. In his first full ride on the USAC circuit in 1965, he finished third in the Indianapolis 500 and won the season driving championship. In 1967, he took on the good ol' boys on the NASCAR circuit, and won the Daytona 500.

In 1969, he came to Indy in Colin Chapman's radically redesigned Lotus and sported one of the best cars in pre-qualifying, but suffered a crash in practice that totaled the car and left him with first- and second-degree burns on his face. Resorting to a back-up car that possessed none of the technical innovations of the Lotus, Andretti qualified in the front row. He matured as a driver in the race—conceding an early lead because his car was overheating, working his way back up the leader board as other racers dropped out with mechanical trouble. On his final lap, before taking the

checkered flag in record time, Andretti thought about his "one very long journey from a displaced persons camp in Italy to the top of the world."

In 1977, he went to the Formula One circuit in Europe and, a year later, fulfilled his boyhood dream of winning the Grand Prix title. He clinched the crown in a bittersweet race at the Italian Grand Prix at Monza (teammate Ronnie Peterson died in the race), just miles from his boyhood home. "I don't know if I could ever describe how much it means to me," he said.

He retired in 1994 as the most versatile, and one of the most beloved, racers ever. "No one taught me how to drive," he said. "I've been driving all of my life. When I got to the big time, I asked guys things, but no one would help me much. So I watched guys and I drove. I learned by doing."

Bob Gibson

"I'VE GOT TO WIN"

On the mound, Bob Gibson was a vision of economy and precision. "He pitches like he's double-parked," said Vin Scully. There was very little of the cat-and-mouse game with Gibson. He was simply a stalker, eyeing the plate with a look of barely controlled menace.

His competitive edge was so finely honed that he refused to fraternize with players from other teams, even keeping a stony distance at All-Star Games. He once claimed to have played tic-tac-toe with his daughter 200 times without once letting her win. "I've always had to win," he said. "I've *got* to win."

Gibson was born in Omaha in 1935, three months after his father had died. He was one of seven kids raised by his mother, a laundry woman, and he survived a spate of childhood illnesses to become the first black to play on the baseball and basketball teams at Omaha's Creighton University.

When Johnny Keane took over as manager of the St. Louis Cardinals in 1961, he put Gibson into his rotation. For the next dozen seasons, he dominated National League hitters. He'd retire in 1975 with 251 wins and two Cy Young Awards, the first pitcher since Walter Johnson to record 3,000 strikeouts. During the 1968 season, he was so overpowering—winning 22 games, striking out 268 hitters and sporting a 1.12 ERA—that he helped push the major league rules committee to lower the pitcher's mound in the following season, to give hitters an added advantage.

But when the pressure was greatest, in pennant races and World Series, he rose to new realms. In the Fall Classic, he posted seven wins in a row, recorded a 1.89 ERA, striking out more than 10 batters per game. In the 1964 World Series, he won the fifth game in 10 innings, 5–2, over the Yankees. On two days rest, Cards manager Johnny Keane brought him back to start Game 7. Gibson didn't have his best stuff, was suffering from a strained arm, but he still struck out nine men in a 7–5 win. "He pitched the last three innings on guts," Keane said.

Gibson won all three of his starts, including Game 7, in the 1967 Series, to carry the Cardinals past the Boston Red Sox for their second title in four years, solidifying his reputation as the era's ultimate big-game pitcher. And he was heroic in the 1968 Series as well, striking out a record 17 Tigers in the opening game, and 10 more in his Game 4 shutout, before losing a Game 7 duel to Mickey Lolich.

Long after Gibson left the game, hitters remembered that scary vision of him on the mound, glaring in toward home plate, determined to succeed on his own terms.

"His ability in baseball," wrote David Halberstam, "did not exist apart from the rest of his being; rather, his ability as a player was an extension of his will as a man. When opposing teams prepared to *battle* Gibson (and that was the right word: battle), they were taking on not just Gibson the pitcher, but Gibson the man."

"His ability
as a ballplayer was an extension
of his will as a man"

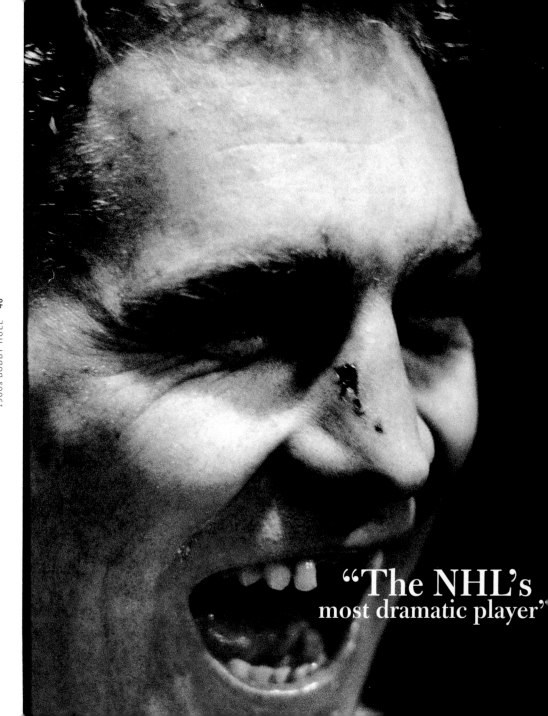

"The NHL's
most dramatic player"

Bobby Hull

THE GOLDEN JET

Born in 1939, in Point Anne, Ontario, Bobby Hull received his first pair of skates for Christmas in 1942. By 1957, he was a star left wing for the Chicago Black Hawks, with a brisk style and temperament that made him a crowd favorite throughout his 23-year career. He was "a statue come alive from the Golden Age of Greece," gushed a Chicago society columnist, "incredibly handsome even without his front teeth." But "statue" seemed an ill-chosen term: More than his slicked-back blond hair, the Golden Jet's blazing speed—clocked at nearly 30 miles per hour—was the source of his nickname. His trademark rushes, capped by his screaming 118 mile-per-hour slapshot, was one of the most thrilling performances professional hockey had ever seen. A 1966 *New York Times* headline asserted simply: "Hull's Success Understandable: Skates Fastest, Shoots Hardest."

Hull played with an almost cheery abandon, his gap-toothed smile in evidence even when heavily shadowed by the game's toughest players. The 22-year-old led the Black Hawks to the Stanley Cup over the Canadiens in 1961, the club's first championship since 1938. By then he had developed one of the sport's first banana blades, and its benefits ultimately forced the league to legislate the degree of curvature allowed. Hull claimed that he scored more goals with the wrist shot than any other.

And there were many. In his third season, 1959–60, he tied for the league lead with 39 goals. He scored 30 or more goals in each of the next 16 seasons, leading the NHL seven times. In 1962, Hull became the third player to reach the 50-goal mark—hockey's magic number, and a record originally set by Maurice "The Rocket" Richard.

Near the end of the 1965-66 season, his Roger Maris-like pursuit of 51 (which he achieved four games after becoming the only player to break the 50 barrier twice) was one of the major sports stories of the year. He finished with 54 goals in 65 games, and would lead the league for the next three years.

In 1972, Hull signed a $1.35-million deal—plus a $1-million signing bonus—with the Winnipeg Jets of the rival World Hockey Association. His defection to the fledgling league gave the WHA instant legitimacy, and marked Hull as "the Joe Namath of hockey." In his first three WHA seasons, he scored 181 goals and won the MVP award twice. He played with the Jets for all seven years of the league's existence, finishing his career back in the NHL with the Hartford Whalers in 1980.

Though he was the NHL's first $100,000 earner and the man who ushered in the big-money era of the '70s, Hull is still best remembered for his speed and his shot. He ended his iron-man run with 610 goals and 560 assists for 1,170 points. "His style of play," wrote E. M. Swift in *Sports Illustrated*, "matched his personality—open, dramatic, uncompromising and utterly joyful."

—David Zivan

Jerry West

THE SHARPSHOOTER

Jerry West doesn't hold a patent on the jump shot, but no one in basketball history was consistently better at scoring from the perimeter than the former Los Angeles Laker star of the '60s and early '70s. The renowned coach Frank McGuire stated flatly, "West is the best shooter I've ever seen."

History will note that West is widely considered among the game's four best guards, a class that includes Michael Jordan, Magic Johnson and Oscar Robertson. He became such an icon that a silhouette of him in action—dribble-driving to his left—adorns the NBA logo.

West averaged 27 points a game over 14 seasons, second among guards to Jordan. Often working the middle ground that is so neglected in the current era of three-point shots and dunks, West devastated opponents with his ability to shoot off the dribble with a lightning release. West also used his quickness to drive around defenders who snuggled up to him with hopes of stopping the jumper.

Though he is best remembered as a shooter, he led the league in assists in 1971–72. Average-sized for a guard at the time—6-foot-3-inches, 180-pounds—he used his speed and long arms to become a ballhawking defender (breaking his nose nine times), earning membership to the All-NBA defensive team four times.

In 1969, West became the only player from a losing team to win an NBA Finals MVP. A year later, he hit the legendary shot from beyond midcourt against the Knicks to send their 1970 Game 3 Finals series game into overtime, though New York won that game and went on to win the championship.

Two years after losing to the Knicks, West would get redemption, teaming with Wilt Chamberlain to win his only NBA title, in 1972. He would have more success with championships in the front office. He helped put together Laker teams that won five NBA titles in the 1980s. As executive vice president of basketball operations for the Lakers, he developed a reputation as perhaps the league's shrewdest judge of talent.

Born in Cheylan, West Virginia (population 500), West played basketball because it was something a small-town kid could do by himself. Perhaps because of his modest roots, West, the second pick in the 1960 NBA draft, often doubted his own ability. "I really played out of fear that I was going to fail," West once said. "If we lost, it was always my fault, and that's a terrible burden to carry around with you."

West's talent and drive made him among the most admired players in the league, and were acknowledged at his retirement ceremony in 1974. "The greatest honor a man can have is the respect and friendship of his peers," said the great Celtics center Bill Russell. "You have that more than any man I know."

—*Mark Rosner*

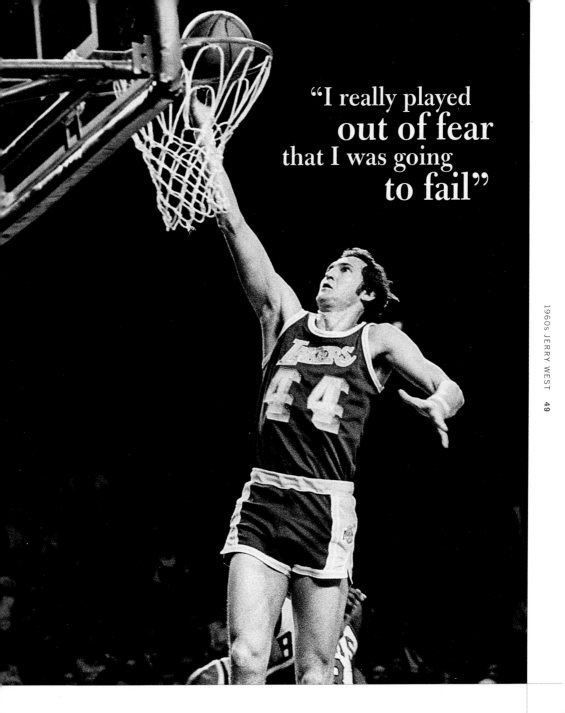

"I really played **out of fear** that I was going **to fail**"

"What famous athlete last died
for a cause bigger than himself?"

Roberto Clemente

"TO BE REMEMBERED"

Roberto Clemente played the game of baseball with a kind of prideful vengeance. The handsome, dark-skinned Puerto Rican's marvelous game never received the credit it deserved, partly because he didn't play in a media capital, and partly because his passion was so frequently misinterpreted as pure vanity. Clemente used the real and perceived slights as the fuel for his fiery, indomitable spirit. "Baseball survives," wrote Jimmy Cannon once, "because guys like Clemente still play it."

Though Mays, Mantle and Aaron got more headlines, Clemente at his best was in the same class. A 12-time All-Star, he batted over .300 in 13 seasons, amassed 3,000 hits, won four National League batting titles and was the NL MVP in 1966. For all that, his ultimate moment of glory didn't come until the 1971 World Series. At age 37 he led the Pirates back from a three-games-to-one deficit to a seven-game win over the Baltimore Orioles, earning MVP honors after hitting .414 with 12 hits in the Series. It was a coming-out party of sorts, as Clemente was finally and publicly regarded as the most complete player in the game.

"The very special thing about Roberto, physically, is his hands," said Tom Seaver. "So very powerful. He stood there, far away from the plate, with that great big long bat, and with those strong hands he controlled it like crazy, hitting pitches on the side of the plate."

To the end, he remained prideful. In the fall of 1972, after the Pirates were eliminated from the playoffs, he complained to friends that he'd been slighted by *Sports Illustrated*, which hadn't put him on the cover after his 3,000th hit. "I want to be remembered as a ballplayer who gave all he had to give," he once said. That line became his epitaph when he was killed in a plane crash on December 31, 1972, on a mission of mercy to help victims of an earthquake in Nicaragua.

After his death, the Baseball Writers Association of America waived the five-year waiting period for the first time since Lou Gehrig's death, and voted Clemente into the Baseball Hall of Fame. On August, 6, 1973, Clemente was inducted along with, among others, his childhood hero, Monte Irvin.

"What famous athlete last died for a cause bigger than himself?" asked Wilfrid Sheed in 1973. "Clemente could sometimes seem like a pest, a nagging narcissist, with only his burningly serious play to deny it. Yet when that plane crashed carrying relief supplies to Nicaragua, we saw what he had meant all along. It was like the old Clemente crashing into the rightfield wall in a losing game: the act of a totally serious man."

Classics

PRO FOOTBALL
1967 NFL Championship The Icemen Cometh

At 13 degrees below zero, with 15 mph winds and a minus-48 wind chill, it was the coldest NFL game on record. On December 31, 1967, the two-time defending champion Green Bay Packers met the Dallas Cowboys in a rematch of the previous season's NFL title game. The teams played in brutal circumstances, on a field that really was frozen tundra, since the 750,000-volt, subterranean heating system below the field went out.

Green Bay jumped ahead to an early 14-0 lead, but the resilient Cowboys fought back to within 14-10 at the half. That's where it stood until the beginning of the fourth quarter, when Dan Reeves threw a halfback-option pass past a stunned Packer secondary to a wide-open Lance Rentzel, who went in for a 50-yard touchdown, putting the Cowboys up 17-14. Green Bay's final drive began on its own 32 with 4:50 remaining. After hitting Donny Anderson to convert a third-and-nine, Bart Starr passed again, hitting Chuck Mercein out of the backfield for a gain of 19, down to the Cowboy 11, with 1:11 left. On the next play, Cowboy tackle Bob Lilly bought the designed fake (guard Gale Gillingham pulling as if to lead the classic Packer power sweep), and Mercein darted through the hole

Lilly left, bringing the Pack down to the Dallas 3. Anderson ran to the one on the next play, giving Green Bay first and goal with 30 seconds left. After two more plays, the Packers used their last time-out, facing a third and goal still at the one.

Instead of calling a relatively safe pass that could be thrown away and would have left time for a game-tying field goal, Lombardi took an epic gamble. On the sidelines during the timeout Starr told him that a quarterback sneak would work. "Then do it," said Lombardi, "and let's get the hell out of here." Jerry Kramer and Ken Bowman double-teamed Cowboy defensive tackle Jethro Pugh, and Starr knifed through the hole that was left, landing in the end zone with 13 seconds left. The Packers had won the "Ice Bowl," 21–17, giving Lombardi his fifth NFL title. After the game, Lombardi acknowledged that the call was a roll of the dice. "I didn't figure the people in the stands wanted to sit around in the cold any longer," he said. "I do have some compassion, though I've been accused of having none."

GOLF
1960 U.S. Open

It was the era of Open Saturday, when the final two rounds of the U.S. Open were played on the same day, testing a man's stamina as much as his golfing skill. As he set out for his final round, on a blazing Saturday afternoon at Cherry Hills in Denver, Arnold Palmer wasn't even on the leader board, standing seven strokes behind leader Mike Souchak and in 15th place. But this would be the day, in Dan Jenkins' words, that "we witnessed the arrival of Nicklaus, the coronation of Palmer, and the end of Hogan." Young Jack Nicklaus, just 20 years old, shot the lowest amateur score ever, a 282. The great Ben Hogan, at 47, made a late charge and had a share of the lead going to the 17th hole, only to falter, finishing in fourth place. But the charismatic chain-smoking Palmer seized the day, drove the green on the 346-yard first hole, birdied each of the first four holes on the way to a 30 on the front nine, and shot a

Putting it on Ice:
Starr's sneak proved the difference in the famed "Ice Bowl."

65, to work all the way back through the field and win his only Open.

PRO FOOTBALL

Super Bowl III

"I personally guarantee it," said Joe Namath and, in so doing, the most visible player of the upstart American Football League had raised the stakes of the third Super Bowl, in January 1969, in which the Baltimore Colts of the National Football League were favored by 19 points. Instead, the country saw the first great upset in Super Bowl history, as Namath played error-free football, read the Colt defense perfectly (audibling frequently), and the Jets outplayed the 14-1 NFL champions, en route to a 16-7 win.

BOXING

1964 Clay-Liston

There was Sonny Liston, the awesome champ, his neck wrapped with towels, delivering his menacing, dead-end stare at the young challenger. And here was the young, pretty, irrepressible Cassius Clay, staring right back at him, growling, "Chump! Now I got you, chump!" The 7-1 underdog walked into the ring in Miami, on February 25, 1964, confident that his elusiveness would confound a champion who was considered unbeatable. Clay proved his mettle in the early rounds, but got in trouble in the fourth, temporarily blinded by the wintergreen and alcohol mixture that the Liston camp was using for liniment on the champ's sore shoulder. But by the end of the fifth round, Clay's vision cleared and he was back on the attack. In the sixth, he peppered the wearying champ with long-range jabs and crisp left hooks. And before the seventh round, Liston's corner threw in the towel, making Liston the first heavyweight champ to lose his title while sitting on his stool since Jess Willard conceded to Jack Dempsey in 1919. The next day, Clay announced he was changing his name to Muhammad Ali, and a new era began.

COLLEGE BASKETBALL

1966 NCAA Championship Game

Texas Western, fielding an all-black starting lineup, knocked off favored Kentucky, featuring an all-white starting lineup, in what many would come to view as a watershed moment, the *"Brown v. Board of Education"* game in college basketball. The final score, 72-65, was closer than the game itself. The Miners took control early and physically dominated Kentucky. While the game was seen years later as a pivotal moment for blacks in basketball, the racial contrast was barely reported at the time. "I don't think I had my head in the sand or anything," said Texas Western coach Don Haskins. "I just never heard the word quota around here. So I played my best players, who happened to be black."

BASEBALL

1960 World Series

The mighty Yankees batted .338 and won Games 2, 3 and 6 by a margin of 35 runs. But at Pittsburgh's Forbes Field, in an unforgettable Game 7, each team took turns pulling off dazzling rallies. The Yankees tied the game in the top of the ninth with two runs, the last on a marvelous baserunning play by Mickey Mantle, who'd singled in the first run. With one out, Mantle at first and pinch-runner Gil McDougald at third, Yogi Berra hit a sharp grounder to first. Rocky Nelson fielded the ball and stepped on the bag, but then Mantle slid back into first, eluding Nelson's late tag, and McDougald scored from third, tying the game at 9-9. Pirate second baseman Bill Mazeroski opened the bottom of the ninth by stroking Ralph Terry's 1-0 slider over the left-field wall to win the game and the Series for Pittsburgh. The Pirates had been outscored 55-27 and had 31 fewer hits in the Series. But for the first time in 35 years, they were world champions.

Champions

THE DECADE OF HARDCOURT DYNASTIES

The two great sporting dynasties of the '60s were so dominant and so powerful, they've become synonymous with the word dynasty.

Beginning in 1964, John Wooden's UCLA Bruins won the NCAA tournament 10 times in 12 years, including a record seven straight from 1967-73.

And in the same era, beginning in 1957, the Boston Celtics were winning 11 out of 13 NBA championships, including a record eight straight from 1959-66. Both teams built their attacks on disciplined, fast-break offenses and pressuring defenses, anchored by dominating big men (Lew Alcindor, then Bill Walton for UCLA, and the irrepressible Bill Russell for the Celtics, player-coach for Boston's last two titles of the '60s).

CITY OF CHAMPIONS.

Los Angeles and Boston had the Bruin and Celtic dynasties, but at the end of the decade, there was no better place to be than New York. Broadway Joe Namath guaranteed, then delivered, the Super Bowl for the Jets in January of 1969. Nine months later, the Amazin' Mets upset the Baltimore Orioles in the '69 World Series. And as workers were cleaning up confetti from that parade, the 1969-70 basketball season was beginning. It would end with Willis Reed and the New York Knicks winning the franchise's first NBA title.

MOST UNLIKELY CHAMPION.

Every year in the NFL playoffs, the networks flash a graphic saying the Oakland Raiders were the first wild-card team to win the Super Bowl. This is technically accurate, but misleading. In 1969, the last year of the American Football League, the Kansas City Chiefs finished 11-3, in second place in the AFL West, but qualified in the league's expanded playoff format. The Chiefs then beat, in succession, the defending world champion Jets, 13-6, at Shea Stadium; the mighty Raiders, 17-7, at Oakland in the AFL's last game; and, finally, the heavily favored Minnesota Vikings, 23-7, in Super Bowl IV in New Orleans. The win was a harbinger of the more complex offenses of the '70s and '80s, and sweet redemption for quarterback Len Dawson and coach Hank Stram, who had been battered by Green Bay in the first Super Bowl.

CLOSE BUT NO CIGAR.

In the 1960s, the Dallas Cowboys built a reputation as a model franchise that simply couldn't win the big one. In their seventh season, 1966, they lost the NFL championship game, 34-27, at home to the Packers.

A year later, they'd lose the NFL title in the famed Ice Bowl. In both 1968 and 1969, Dallas won the NFL's Capitol Division, only to be eliminated in the first round of the playoffs by Cleveland.

Champions

	College Basketball	Pro Basketball NBA	Pro Basketball ABA	Hockey NHL
'60	OHIO STATE	CELTICS		CANADIENS
'61	CINCINNATI	CELTICS		BLACK HAWKS
'62	CINCINNATI	CELTICS		MAPLE LEAFS
'63	LOYOLA, IL	CELTICS		MAPLE LEAFS
'64	UCLA	CELTICS		MAPLE LEAFS
'65	UCLA	CELTICS		CANADIENS
'66	TEXAS WESTERN	CELTICS		CANADIENS
'67	UCLA	76ERS		MAPLE LEAFS
'68	UCLA	CELTICS	PIPERS	CANADIENS
'69	UCLA	CELTICS	OAKS	CANADIENS

NOTES: **Pro Football:** AFL and NFL signed merger agreement before 1966 season, and played the first Super Bowl in the January following that season. Champions are listed in the calendar year of the regular season. **College Football:** Champions are mythical national champion, as voted by sportswriters in the Associated Press poll and by coaches in the United Press International poll. **Pro Basketball:** American Basketball Association began play in 1967-68 season.

Baseball MLB	College Football	Pro Football NFL	AFL
PIRATES	MINNESOTA	EAGLES	OILERS
YANKEES	ALABAMA	PACKERS	OILERS
YANKEES	USC	PACKERS	TEXANS
DODGERS	TEXAS	BEARS	CHARGERS
CARDINALS	ALABAMA	BROWNS	BILLS
DODGERS	ALABAMA (AP) MICH. ST. (UPI)	PACKERS	BILLS
ORIOLES	NOTRE DAME	PACKERS	
CARDINALS	USC	PACKERS	
TIGERS	OHIO STATE	JETS	
METS	TEXAS	CHIEFS	

Coaches

"Winning isn't everything, it's the only thing."
—*The famous quote often attributed to Vince Lombardi, though UCLA coach Red Sanders is cited (in Bartlett's Familiar Quotations) as the person who said it first. Lombardi later said that if he did say it, what he meant to say was, "Winning isn't everything, but trying to win is."*

"Only three things can happen when you pass the football. And two of them are bad."
—*Ohio State's Woody Hayes, who popularized his "three yards and a cloud of dust" offensive attack in the 60s.*

WHEN GIANTS WALKED THE SIDELINES

Vince Lombardi, who had been one of Fordham's famed "Seven Blocks of Granite" linemen, took over the Green Bay Packers in 1959 and in the '60s led them to five NFL championships (and the first two Super Bowl victories). Along the way, he created an aura of football dominance so powerful that the NFL ultimately named its Super Bowl champions trophy after him.

Forty years after he took over in Green Bay, Lombardi's offensive philosophy, simple, power football, relying more on physical superiority and execution rather than trickery or razzle-dazzle, remains a cornerstone of any successful pro offense. Power sweeps are no longer the meat and potatoes of football attacks, but Lombardi's underlying contribution—the superb execution of pulling guards toward the point of attack, and using double-teaming and cross blocks to confuse and exploit the opposition's first line of defense—remain part of football's strategic liturgy.

He was football's most famous taskmaster, torturing his Packers in training camp with his feared grass drills, and treating his players like wayward boys in an orphan home, who needed both mental and moral discipline. "If you cheat on the practice field, you'll cheat in the game," he said, "and if you cheat in the game, you'll cheat the rest of your life."

While Lombardi dominated the sideline, Red Auerbach became the most commanding presence in pro basketball arenas. The crafty, inimitable Brooklynite became synonymous with winning, leading his Celtics to nine NBA titles in his last 10 seasons as a head coach. Few coaches ever took greater joy in triumph; Auerbach's traditional victory cigar, lit after a Celtic win was in the bag, was described by Bob Cousy as "the single most arrogant act in all of sports."

One of the ironies is that after Auerbach retired, the Celtics were often associated with great white players—Larry Bird, Dave Cowens, Kevin McHale. Some even suggested that there was a grand plan on Boston's part to remain the whitest team in the league. That conveniently omitted Auerbach's contributions to integrating the NBA. Boston was the first team to draft an African-American player (Chuck Cooper in 1950), the first to field an all-black starting five (1964) and the first to hire a black head coach (Bill Russell, in 1966). "He was no leader of civil rights," said Cousy. "But show him a polka-dotted seven-footer who can dunk and he'll put him on the team. He was completely one-dimensional—his entire life was win."

Influences

THE CONSUMMATE POLITICIAN

On January 26, 1960, Pete Rozelle, the 33-year-old general manager for the Los Angeles Rams, was named commissioner of the National Football League, a compromise choice selected on the 23rd ballot. At the time, the 12-team league's offices were in suburban Philadelphia, and pro football was still a distant second to baseball in the affections of the American public (a 1961 Gallup poll showed 34 percent of Americans naming baseball as their favorite sport, 21 percent naming football).

The underestimated Rozelle simply revolutionized modern sports over the next decade. Moving the league's offices to New York City, to be closer to the media centers that were integral to the league's health, Rozelle pushed through a visionary revenue-sharing agreement (which allowed small-market franchises such as Green Bay to compete on equal footing with the New Yorks and Chicagos of the league) whose cornerstone was a league-wide television contract that would soon enough become the envy of the entire sports world.

Jack Kent Cooke, who owned the Washington Redskins and entertained the cream of D.C.'s power elite in his owner's box, called Rozelle "as skillful a politician as I have met in my life. His capacity to conjure up agreement is sometimes nothing short of miraculous. He is the consummate politician."

Rozelle understood that the NFL was "selling an experience" to its fan base, a new generation of middle-class workaday Americans who had fewer cares and more disposable income in the postwar years.

Rozelle presided over the potentially divisive competition with Lamar Hunt and the American Football League, signing a merger agreement in 1966 that led to a joint draft and the Super Bowl, and the full merger in 1970. Two years later, in another Gallup poll, 36 percent of Americans said football was their favorite sport, while only 21 percent chose baseball.

Top Of The News:

Every institution in America is being questioned, yet the world of sports continues to grow nad college football celebrates its 100th anniversary. A new football league rises up to challenge the NFL and a new basketball league takes on the NBA. By the end of the decade, a Gallup poll shows that pro football has replaced baseball as the most popular sport in the land.

MOVIES

It's a bad decade for baseball and football movies, but Paul Newman (in his breakthrough role) and Jackie Gleason shine in *The Hustler* and, in 1969, Robert Redford is convincing in *Downhill Racer*. Based on the novel by Walter Tevis, *The Hustler* tells the story of "Fast" Eddie Felson, a pool shark who makes his way across the country, intent on taking down billiards legend Minnesota Fats. In *Downhill Racer*, Redford—doing most of his own stunts—plays self-centered American skiing hope Davis Chappellet, who clashes with his coach (Gene Hackman) while fighting for the gold medal in the downhill. Charlton Heston played an aging quarterback for the New Orleans Saints in 1969's *Number One*, whose main claim to fame was a guest role by Saints head coach Tom Fears.

READING LIST

The decade is highlighted by two intimate glimpses into the world of professional football. First there's participatory journalist George Plimpton's *Paper Lion*, a vivid sketch of what a professional football team looks

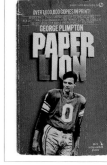

like to an Everyman interloper. The flip side is the view from inside from one of the gladiators, Jerry Kramer's *Instant Replay*, co-written with Dick Schaap. The memoir of a season with the Green Bay Packers presents almost harrowing images of the physical, emotional, and psychological toll exacted by training camp, and the long season that follows.

The big baseball book of the decade is a big baseball book: *Macmillan's Official Baseball Encyclopedia*, the first definitive book on the statistical history of the sport. Eliot Asinof's *Eight Men Out* provides the truest look at the events leading up to and including the Black Sox scandal at the 1919 World Series. Lawrence Ritter's *In the Glory of Their Times* is the first and best of many books in baseball's oral history.

But the two most memorable pieces of the decade are both in *The New Yorker*. "Hub Fans Bid Kid Adieu," by John Updike, takes the measure of Ted Williams' final game at Fenway Park, and John McPhee's *A Sense of Where You Are* is an intimate profile of Princeton all-American Bill Bradley that originally ran as a piece in the magazine.

POLITICS

More than ever before, the real world intersects with sports. Pete Rozelle decides the NFL should go ahead and play games just two days after President Kennedy is assassinated, and is roundly criticized for it. (He later describes the decision to play the games as the biggest mistake of his 29-year career as commissioner.) Five years later, in 1968, the Mexico City Olympics' most

ROBERT REDFORD GENE HACKMAN CAMILLA SPARV DOWNHILL RACER

incredible athletic feat (Bob Beamon's world-record long jump) is overshadowed by its most compelling statement of protest (John Carlos' and Tommie Smith's raised, black-gloved fists of salute during the playing of the National Anthem). Sports is no longer just an escape, but also a reflection of society.

TELEVISION

In an episode of *The Munsters* that first aired on April 8, 1965, Herman is showing Eddie how to hit a baseball when he smacks one that travels eight blocks, hitting Dodgers manager Leo Durocher in the head. Durocher, dazed but impressed, gives Herman a tryout, but the hapless giant inadvertently does $75,000 damage to Dodgers Stadium and terrifies the team, which begs assignment to the minor leagues en masse if Munster is signed.

FASHION

The Denver Broncos get off to an ignominious start with their ill-fated brown and yellow ensemble. Brown helmet, yellow jersey, brown pants, and socks with alternating vertical brown and yellow stripes. In August 1962, prior to an intrasquad game, the Broncos throw the socks into a bonfire to celebrate the end of a blighted era.

All across football there is a move toward more color in football uniforms. The Minnesota Vikings wear purple pants for away games, the Kansas City Chiefs break out fire-engine red pants for road games, and even the stodgy old Pittsburgh Steelers come up with gold accents on the shoulders of their white road jerseys.

The same trend is seen in baseball, where in 1963, the Kansas City Athletics introduce gold sleeveless uniforms with green shirts underneath, the first time in nearly 30 years a major league team has worn anything other than white uniforms for home games. A year later, Chicago White Sox road uniforms change from gray to light blue, and two expansion teams in 1969—the Seattle Pilots and the Montreal Expos— also wear blue road uniforms.

IMPRESSIONS OF THE '60S
From ESPN's Charley Steiner:

The Sixties. The decade of Love. And Haight. And social revolution. And conscience. And gloves.

...The gloves worn by Muhammad Ali, who changed only everything about what athletes were supposed to be. An athlete, a showman, a salesman, a social force, a political leader, the conscience of a generation, not because he wanted to be, but was destined to be. A hero of the black inner city and the white college campus. When he put on his gloves, he was an artist in the ring, like no other heavyweight before. Or since.

...Tommie Smith and John Carlos, made their athletic mark with their feet and their social contribution, wearing black gloves on their clenched fists after Smith won the gold medal and Carlos, the bronze in Mexico City. An act of conscience and a call for black power, within months of the murders of Martin Luther King and Robert Kennedy.

...And the glove of the lithe center fielder Curt Flood, who told the Cardinals and the Phillies and baseball, hell no, he wouldn't go. Again, an act of conscience. "I do not feel that I am a piece of property to be bought and sold." He would be a martyr for major leaguers forever.

...Ali, Smith, Carlos and Flood. Symbols of the Sixties.

Love and Haight.

"Where have you gone, Joe DiMaggio? A nation turns its lonely eyes to you"
—Paul Simon, *singing about lost innocence in Mrs. Robinson*

Debuts and Exits

1960 | The two-point option on points after touchdown, in the American Football League.
Exit - **Friday Night Fights** is canceled by NBC.

1961 | The Los Angeles Angels (who later move to Anaheim) and **Washington Senators** (who become the Texas Rangers) in Major League Baseball.
The fiberglass pole in pole vaulting.

1962 | **Dodger Stadium,** with a 6-3 Dodger loss to the Reds.
The Houston Colt .45s (who later change their name to the Astros) and the **New York Mets** in baseball.

1963 | The Pro Football Hall of Fame in Canton, Ohio.
NFL Properties, the licensing arm of the NFL.
Instant replay, used by CBS during the Army-Navy game.

1964 | **The Sports Illustrated swimsuit issue.**
The soccer-style kicker in pro football, with Buffalo's signing of Pete Gogolak of Cornell.

1965 | **Indoor baseball,** with the opening of the Astrodome in Houston.
The International Swimming Hall of Fame in Ft. Lauderdale, Florida.

1966 | **The Atlanta Braves,** who move from Milwaukee.
Black head coaches in the NBA, with the Celtics' naming Bill Russell their player-coach.
Merger agreement between the NFL and AFL ending six years of player bidding wars.

1967 | The American Basketball Association, with the Oakland Oaks beating the Anaheim Amigos, 132–129.
Exit - **The dunk in college basketball.**
The first Super Bowl officially titled the NFL-AFL World Championship Game until 1969.
The Fosbury Flop in the high jump, as popularized by Dick Fosbury.

1968 | **The North American Soccer League.**
The Open Era in tennis, as professionals become eligible for Grand Slam
The U.S. Hockey Hall of Fame in Eveleth, Minnesota.
The Naismith Memorial Basketball Hall of Fame, in Springfield, Massachusetts.

1969 | Kansas City Royals, Seattle Pilots (who become the **Milwaukee Brewers),**
San Diego Padres, and **Montreal Expos** join Major League Baseball.
Divisional play and the League Championship Series in major league baseball.

Stats

112

Record number of games it took Pancho Gonzales to beat Charles Pasarell at Wimbledon in 1969.

$18,000,000

Amount paid in indemnities by the American Football League, to merge with the NFL in 1966.

66

Number of yards Jim Marshall of the Vikings ran in the wrong direction for a safety against the 49ers in 1964.

$50,000

Rights fee CBS paid to telecast 1960 Winter Olympics from Squaw Valley.

1,815

Number of hits Musial had on the road.

00:50

Amount of time left in New York Jets–Oakland Raiders game November 17, 1968, when NBC cut away from game to begin airing its Sunday night movie, Heidi. Jets were leading 32-29 when game went off air; Raiders rallied to win, 43-32.

$40

Price of a season ticket for the Minnesota Vikings in their inaugural season, 1961.

1,815

Number of career hits Stan Musial had at home when he retired in 1963.

Wilt Chamberlain's **100** points ▪ No. **99**, Wayne Gretzky ▪ The Drive, John Elway's **98**-yard march ▪ Don Larsen's **97**-pitch World Series perfect game ▪ Ty Cobb's **96** stolen bases ▪ Cal Ripken's **95**-game errorless streak at shortstop ▪ The baseball strike of '**94** ▪ Chris Webber calls timeout in the '93 NCAA title game ▪ San Francisco goes **92** yards to win Super Bowl XXIII ▪ Mike Tyson's **91**-second knockout of Michael Spinks ▪ Grover Cleveland Alexander's **90** shutouts ▪ Billy Cannon's **89**-yard punt return to beat Ole Miss ▪ UCLA's **88**-game win streak in basketball ▪ Bill Bradley's **87** points in the Final Four ▪ Cary Middlecoff's **86**-foot putt at The Masters ▪ Sugar Ray Robinson's **85**-0 amateur record ▪ Jimmy Connors' **84** Wimbledon match wins ▪ North Carolina State upsets Houston in '**83** ▪ "With the **82**nd selection, the San Francisco 49ers draft Joe Montana" ▪ Sam Snead's **81** career PGA tournament wins ▪ The **80**-match rivalry between Martina Navratilova and Chris Evert ▪ Emlen Tunnell's **79** career interceptions ▪ The century's last Triple Crown winner, Affirmed in '**78** ▪ No. **77**, Red Grange ▪ Teemu Selanne's **76** goals as a rookie ▪ Ali vs. Frazier in the '**75** Thrilla in Manila ▪ Marcus Allen's **74**-yard Super Bowl touchdown run ▪ The Bears' **73**-0 title game rout of the Redskins ▪ Ricky Williams' **72** rushing touchdowns at Texas ▪ Nebraska-Oklahoma in '**71** ▪ Mark McGwire's **70** home runs ▪ The Amazin' Mets of '**69** ▪ Mexico City in '**68** ▪ Earl Webb's **67** doubles in a season ▪ Sammy Sosa's **66** home runs ▪ "**65** Toss Power Trap" ▪ O.J. Simpson's **64**-yard run to beat UCLA ▪ Tom Dempsey's and Jason Elam's **63**-yard field goals ▪ Margaret Court's **62** major championships ▪ Roger Maris' **61** homers ▪ The Last **60**-Minute Man, Chuck Bednarik ▪ Orel Hershiser's **59** consecutive scoreless innings ▪ Miami, Florida's **58**-game home winning streak ▪ Cal's **57**-yard kickoff return to beat Stanford ▪ Joe DiMaggio's **56**-game hitting streak ▪ Eddie Robinson's **55** seasons coaching Grambling ▪ Willie Mays' catch in '**54** ▪ Ben Hogan's three majors in '**53** ▪ Gordie Howe, playing in the NHL at age **52** ▪ Bobby Thomson's homer in '**51** ▪ Maurice Richard, and the first **50**-goal season ▪ Rocky Marciano's **49**-0 career record ▪ Doug Flutie's **48**-yard "Miracle in Miami" pass ▪ Oklahoma's **47**-game winning streak in football ▪ The Bears' **46** defense ▪ The Houston Colt .**45**s ▪ Bill Walton's **44** points in the NCAA finals ▪ Car No. **43**, Richard Petty ▪ No. **42**, Jackie Robinson ▪ Jack Chesbro's **41**-win season ▪ Ernie Nevers' **40**-point game ▪ Barry Sanders' **39**-touchdown season at Oklahoma State ▪ Don Budge's Grand Slam in '**38** ▪ The **37**-foot Green Monster ▪ Harvey Haddix retires the first **36** batters ▪ Washington's **35**-point second quarter in Super Bowl XXII ▪ Northwestern's **34**-game losing streak ▪ The Lakers' **33**-game win streak ▪ No. **32**, Jim Brown ▪ Secretariat's **31**-length win in the Belmont Stakes ▪ Bobby Jones' Grand Slam in '**30** ▪ "Harvard Beats Yale, **29**-29" ▪ Alabama's **28** bowl victories ▪ Dean Smith's **27** NCAA tournaments ▪ Baseball's longest game, **26** innings ▪ Joe Louis' **25** successful title defenses ▪ The Yankees' **24** World Series titles ▪ No. **23**, Michael Jordan ▪ Jerry Rice's **22**-touchdown reception season ▪ The Orioles' 0-**21** start ▪ Jack Nicklaus' **20** majors ▪ The Black Sox scandal of '**19** ▪ Mickey Mantle's **18** World Series homers ▪ The Dolphins' perfect **17**-0 season ▪ Citation's and Cigar's **16**-race win streaks ▪ Hank Aaron's **15** thirty-homer seasons ▪ Dick "Night Train" Lane's **14**-interception season ▪ Bob Gibson's **13**-shutout season ▪ The Packers' **12** NFL championships ▪ Byron Nelson's **11** consecutive tournament wins ▪ Nadia Comaneci's perfect **10** ▪ Carl Lewis' **9** Olympic gold medals ▪ The Celtics' **8** straight NBA titles ▪ Nolan Ryan's **7** no-hitters ▪ Kareem Abdul-Jabbar's **6** MVPs ▪ Carl Hubbell's **5** consecutive All-Star Game strikeouts ▪ The **4** Horsemen of Notre Dame ▪ No. **3**, Babe Ruth ▪ Gene Sarazen's double-eagle **2** ▪ "We're No. **1** !"